D0853936

DOGS SET III

Scottish Terriers

Bob Temple
ABDO Publishing Company

visit us at
www.abdopub.com

Published by ABDO Publishing Company, 4940 Viking Drive, Suite 622, Edina, Minnesota 55435.

Printed in the United States.

Edited by Paul Joseph

Photo credits: Peter Arnold, Inc.; Ron Kimball; Animals Animals

Library of Congress Cataloging-in-Publication Data

Temple, Bob.
      Scottish terriers / Bob Temple
           p. cm. — (Dogs. Set III)
      Summary: Describes the physical characteristics of Scotties and discusses how to care for them as pets.
      ISBN 1-57765-421-8
      1. Scottish terrier—Juvenile literature. [1. Scottish terrier. 2. Dogs. 3. Pets] I. Title.

SF429.S4 T46 2000
636.755—dc21
                    00-036191

Contents

Where Dogs Come From

Dogs have been faithful **companions** to humans for thousands of years. Many of them are family pets, but some of them have jobs to do, too. Some dogs help their owners by herding sheep or helping to hunt.

One dog that has often worked for its owner is the Scottish Terrier. They are very good at digging and tunneling. They were used to chase foxes, ferret, and other small creatures into their underground homes.

Dogs come from a species of animals called Canidae, from the Latin word canis, which means "dog." Foxes and wolves are also members of this family of animals.

Opposite page: Scottish Terriers are related to the Wolf.

The Scottie

Scottish Terriers are often called "Scotties" for short. Scotties are from the Terrier group of dogs. While they are not very big, they are strong, confident dogs that are not afraid of much. It is often said that the Scottish Terrier believes he is a giant! They have a sturdy body, a muscular neck, and very short legs.

The Scottie originally came from an area called Aberdeen, Scotland. It was first called the Aberdeen Terrier. The **breed** came to America in 1883. It became very popular in the United States when President Franklin Roosevelt brought his Scottie, Fala, to live with him in the White House.

Opposite page: President Roosevelt petting his Scottie, Fala.

What They're Like

Scotties make good family pets. They are playful and active, and they are very protective of their human families. They make good watchdogs. If they spend a lot of time with people when they are puppies, they will be more friendly when they are grown up. Some Scotties get stubborn and ornery when they get older.

The Scottie will love its family, but it won't need constant attention. They can be independent, too. Scotties love to play ball games with their owners. They like to take walks. They are good with children who treat them kindly. Scotties may snap at children who tease them.

Opposite page: Scotties make good family pets.

8

Coat and Color

Scotties have a thick, wiry **coat** that is kept short on their backs and grows longer on their sides, like a skirt. Under the thick outer coat is a soft undercoat that keeps the Scottie warm in bad weather.

Longer hair above their eyes and around their mouths makes it appear like they have bushy eyebrows and a beard. Scotties are usually black or grayish black. They can have some lighter patches of fur on their chests, too.

Opposite page: The Scottie has a thick outer coat.

Size

Scotties have short, compact bodies. They usually weigh between 18 and 22 pounds (8.2 to 10 kg) and are about 10 inches tall (25.4 cm). The males are usually a little bigger than the females.

Their bodies are long and thick and their legs are very short. They have a long **muzzle** and large teeth. They have dark, almond-shaped eyes, and a black nose. Their tails are straight or slightly curved. Their ears are pointed and stand up straight.

Opposite page: Scotties have thick bodies, but very short legs.

Care

Even though the hair on a Scottie's back is short, it still needs to be brushed regularly. A strong steel comb is the best tool for taking care of this fur, but a stiff brush works, too. The Scottie's **coat** needs to be combed three times a week. Also, Scottie's need to be trimmed about twice a year. The Scottie's eyes, ears, teeth, and nails should be checked regularly to make sure they are healthy.

Scotties should be kept indoors. They are small enough to live in an apartment, but they need lots of outdoor exercise, too. It's a good idea to be outside with your dog and have it on a leash. Scotties can play alone in a fenced yard, but you should make sure they can't dig out under the fence. Since they were once used to hunt animals underground, Scotties love to dig! They like to live in a cooler climate if possible.

You should make sure to take your dog to the **veterinarian** at least once a year. He will need shots to make sure he doesn't get diseases that are dangerous to dogs, like **distemper** and **rabies**.

The Scottie needs a lot of outdoor exercise.

Feeding

Your Scottie can only be a happy member of the family if he is getting the right **nutrition**. Good food, and the right amount of it, will keep your Scottie healthy.

When you buy your Scottie puppy, you should ask the breeder what kind of dog food the puppy has been getting. You should keep feeding the puppy the same food in the beginning. Any changes to his diet should be made gradually. Your **veterinarian** can help you pick a food that is right for your dog.

Puppies usually get fed twice a day. As your dog gets older and becomes an adult, they usually get fed only once per day. Clean, fresh water should be available at all times. *Opposite page: In order for your Scottie to have a happy, healthy life it must be on a proper diet.*

Things They Need

Regular exercise is important for Scotties, just as it is for all dogs. Scotties love to be taken on walks. They also like to go outside and play a game of fetch with a ball, bone, or stick. They should also have some chew toys to help keep them from getting bored. The right kind of chew toy will also help keep your dog's teeth healthy.

Scotties, like all dogs, need to be trained. Learning to sit, stay, and lay down not only makes them a better member of the family, it also helps keep them safe. Scotties need to be trained gently, though. They are sensitive dogs and don't like to be punished.

Dogs should always wear a collar with an identification tag that includes the owners name, address, and phone number. This way, if he gets

lost, the person who finds him can call the owner. Some cities also require dogs to have a **license**. Many dogs also wear a tag that says they have gotten their **rabies** shot.

Scotties love to be outside and have fun.

Puppies

Scotties can have as many as five puppies in a **litter**. Sometimes, a Scottie's fur will change color in the first few weeks after it is born. Scotties, like all other dogs, are **mammals**. This means they drink milk from their mother's body when they are first born. After about four to six weeks, they can be fed soft puppy food.

Puppies need more shots than adult dogs. If you buy a Scottie puppy, you should take him to the **veterinarian** as soon as possible to help him get started on the right foot!

When they are born, their ears are small and don't point up. After about 6-8 weeks, the ears point up. In some Scotties, the ears droop a little,

Opposite page: Scottie puppies need a lot of care and attention.

so their owners use a brace to keep them up until
they stay up on their own. If they are healthy,
Scotties live to be 12 to 15 years old.

Glossary

breed: a group of dogs that share the same appearance and characteristics.

coat: the hair that covers a dog's body.

companion: one that keeps company with another; a friend.

distemper: a contagious disease that dogs sometimes get. It is caused by a virus.

license (LIE-sense): a tag worn by a dog indicating it has been registered with a city.

litter: the group of puppies a dog has in one pregnancy.

mammal: warm-blooded animals that feed their babies milk from the mother's body.

muzzle: the jaws and nose of a dog; snout.

nutrition (new-TRISH-un): food; nourishment.

rabies: a serious virus that is very dangerous to dogs.

veterinarian (VET-er-in-AIR-ian): your dog's doctor; also called a vet.

Internet Sites

American Kennel Club of America
http://www.akc.org
Find tips for buying a Scottie puppy, including breeder references, and information about the club at this site. Read the American Kennel Club's standard for the breed, find out about health problems common to Scotties, and find regional clubs to join, too.

The Scottish Terrier Home Page
http://w3.ag.uiuc.edu/VJR/scottie.html
Learn about Scotties in history and find out about Scotties in literature at this site. You can find out about clubs to join and even look at some Scottie-related merchandise.

Index

FRANKFORD